THE CHILTER AND THE THAMES VALLEY

Paul Felix

ALAN SUTTON
in association with Berkshire Books

First published in the United Kingdom in 1992 by
Alan Sutton Publishing, Phoenix Mill, Far Thrupp, Stroud,
Gloucestershire

British Library Cataloguing in Publication Data

Felix, Paul
  Chilterns and the Thames Valley
  I. Title
  914.2504

ISBN 0–7509–0095–4

Typeset in 8/10 Bembo.
Typesetting and origination by
Alan Sutton Publishing Limited.
Printed in Great Britain by
The Guernsey Press Company Limited,
Guernsey, Channel Islands.

THE CHILTERNS AND THE THAMES VALLEY

The Chiltern Hills and the valley of the river Thames together contain some
of the most attractive scenery in the south of England. These beautiful
photographs by Paul Felix take us from the upland farms and beechwoods to
the pretty villages and towns of the valleys. On the way we take a look at the
crafts and industries of the area, dominated now, as of old, by the availability
of local timber and also at the river, and the way that its presence has
influenced local architecture and leisure activities.

ABINGDON

The elegant spire of St Helen's Church, reflected in the waters of the Thames on a summer's day. Abingdon used to be the county town of Berkshire but in the nineteenth century this accolade passed to Reading and, in more recent county boundary changes, Abingdon found itself part of Oxfordshire.

ABINGDON

A quiet backwater of the Thames near the town centre. Medieval Abingdon drew its prosperity from the cloth trade and more recently its biggest employer was the famous MG car factory which closed in the late 1970s. In spite of its closeness to Oxford the town retains a life and identity of its own.

AMERSHAM

The cricket ground at Amersham below the rolling hills of the Chilterns. Although a commuter town, at weekends local sportsmen put on their 'whites' and a village atmosphere prevails.

AMERSHAM

Timber-framed buildings and St Mary's Church, which is noted for its monuments to local families. Externally the church is mainly Victorian but inside there are many interesting features dating from the Norman period onwards.

AMERSHAM

The Town Hall was built in 1682 by Sir William Drake, a member of one of Amersham's best-known families. Sited on the old coaching route from Aylesbury to London, it now occupies a quieter spot following the building of a bypass round the town.

AMERSHAM

An autumn day in the Chilterns near Amersham as the fields are made ready for next year's crops. In spite of modern developments around the new parts of Amersham there is still a strong farming influence in the area.

ASTON

A family of swans
enjoy a quiet part of the
Thames at Aston, a riverside
hamlet near Henley. Even
when summer visitors take
over the more popular
stretches of the Thames,
Aston remains a peaceful
backwater.

AYLESBURY

The Market Square in
Aylesbury, the county town
of Buckinghamshire, with a
Clock Tower designed by the
Victorian architect, Brandon.
The Square has many
interesting features including a
monument to John Hampden,
a prominent Parliamentarian.

AYLESBURY

A row of cottages in Castle Street, set between the busy ring road and the quieter inner centre of the town. Although Aylesbury is the county town and has expanded greatly in recent years it still manages to retain a market town atmosphere.

AYLESBURY

Church Street has some fine buildings including Ceely House, now part of the Buckinghamshire County Museum, and built in the eighteenth century. At the top of the street can be seen the parish church of St Mary.

AYLESBURY

The parish church of St Mary dates from the thirteenth and early fourteenth centuries but was restored by Sir Gilbert Scott in Victorian times. It is notable for its strange little spire built on top of the original tower and also for a fine Norman font.

BEACONSFIELD

A row of shops in the main street of the Old Town, once the busy London to Oxford road. The opening of the M40 in recent years transformed the town, returning it to the pace it enjoyed in the days of the stage coach.

BEACONSFIELD

Bekonscot model village opened in 1929 in the garden of a house and has been seen by over ten million visitors. The model, at a scale of one inch to the foot, has moving trains and raises money for local good causes.

BEACONSFIELD

The Chiltern area is rich in craftsmen but stickmaker Theo Fossel of Beaconsfield is known the world over. He demonstrates and lectures abroad, particularly in the United States, and is the author of a standard book on stickmaking.

BRADENHAM

The beechwoods of the Chilterns are one of the area's main features and for many years have provided work for local people, in the cottage industries of chair bodging (using turned wood) and charcoal burning. Now the more managed woodlands provide timber for the nearby furniture factories.

BRADENHAM

Cricket on the village green at Bradenham in front of the seventeenth-century manor house which was the boyhood home of Victorian Prime Minister, Benjamin Disraeli.

BOURNE END

Bourne End, now a large sprawling village, lies on the banks of the Thames between Marlow and Maidenhead. It attracts many summer visitors, particularly to its well-known sailing club. Dinghy sailing on the Thames is a popular pastime.

BRAY

The riverside village of Bray has for years attracted the rich and famous. The Bray lock is one of the best kept on the Thames and each year its displays of flowers draw admiration from its many visitors.

BRILL

The windmill at Brill is a well-known landmark on the extreme northern edge of the Chilterns. Built around 1680 it is one of the finest examples of its type in the country and was used by local farmers for grinding their corn. The mill is now maintained by local enthusiasts.

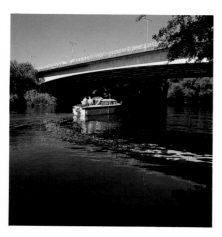

BRAY

The bridge carrying the M4 motorway over the Thames near Bray could not be described as the most elegant bridge over the river but traffic on the river below can pass quietly in a world of its own.

CHALFONT ST GILES

This tollhouse once stood beside the London Road at High Wycombe and was moved to the Chiltern Open Air Museum in the grounds of Newland Park to take its place among other historic buildings. Most of the exhibits have been moved from other sites and include an early furniture factory.

CHALFONT ST GILES

The parish church of St Giles stands not far from the green in this busy village. Built of local flint, it has a particularly pretty carved doorway and a rich array of fourteenth-century paintings. John Milton who lived in a nearby cottage probably worshipped here and possibly also Captain Cook who was a visitor to a nearby estate, The Vache. Circus man Bertram Mills is buried in the churchyard.

CHALFONT ST GILES

This simple cottage, now a museum, was the home of John Milton, one of the country's greatest poets. He arrived in 1665, the year of the Great Plague of London, and can never have seen the cottage for by this time he was blind. It was here that he wrote *Paradise Regained*.

CHEQUERS

The country residence of British prime ministers. Built on a site mentioned in the Domesday Book, the house, which dates back in parts to the sixteenth century, was presented to the nation by Lord Lee of Fareham in 1917. The house can be seen across the fields from the road and nearby footpaths.

CLIVEDEN

Cliveden, one of the most impressive country houses in the land, was for many years the home of the Astor family. Although the main part of the house is now a hotel, some rooms and the extensive grounds are open to the public. The views from the gardens are among the most spectacular in the Thames Valley.

CLIVEDEN

This highly ornamental building at the front of the house is a dovecote. The gardens show many influences, with styles ranging from those of the eighteenth century to the present day.

CLIVEDEN REACH

An impressive view of the
Thames below Cliveden
House, seen here during the
autumn with the colours of
the changing leaves reflected
in the water.

CLIVEDEN

One of the most extravagant
features of the gardens at
Cliveden is the sumptuous
French fountain made for
Lord Astor by Ralph Waldo
Story. The house itself was
built by Sir Charles Barry,
architect of the Houses of
Parliament.

COOKHAM

Cookham Moor, set between
Cookham and Cookham Rise,
has for many years attracted
artists. The fine brick-built
bridge, a gift from a local
benefactor, helped people to
travel by foot over the once
marshy moor but with the
coming of heavier traffic a
new road was built, bypassing
the bridge altogether.

COOKHAM

The riverside church of the
Holy Trinity has attracted
visitors for many years. The
village also has a Stanley
Spencer Gallery dedicated to
the artist who lived and
painted here until his death in
1959. His painting
Resurrection shows the dead
rising from their graves in
Cookham churchyard.

COOMBE HILL

This memorial to those who fell in the Boer War is at Coombe Hill, the highest point on the Chilterns and a spot with magnificent views across the vale of Aylesbury. This bleak hill is a favourite haunt of kite fliers.

CRAZIES HILL

Rebecca's Well, built more than a century ago over the site of a spring to enable local people to draw water more easily. The well, in woods near the village, still has a supply of fresh water.

CRAZIES HILL

Summerfield House was once the Town Hall at Henley-on-Thames, but at the turn of the century it was moved, brick by brick, and rebuilt here as a private house. It was recently renovated and a large lake made in the grounds, making it one of the most impressive houses in the area.

DINTON

Dinton Hall with its Tudor gables and tall chimneys stands close to the church of St Peter and St Paul. This small hamlet lies just off the Thame road not far from Aylesbury.

DORCHESTER

The Abbey Church of
St Peter and St Paul
overshadows the village of
Dorchester, one of the most
historic spots in the area. Here
was the site of the Cathedral
of Wessex before the Norman
Conquest, set close to the spot
where the rivers Thames and
Thame meet.

ELLESBOROUGH

A row of whitewashed farm
cottages seen across the fields
on an evening in late summer
as shadows fall across the
ripening crops.

ELLESBOROUGH

Appearing over the roofs of
this row of cottages is the
tower of the church of
St Peter and St Paul. The
church, known locally as 'the
Prime Minister's Church',
because of its proximity to
Chequers, has been used by
many visiting heads of state
over the years.

ETON

Eton College, seen here across
the Thames, was founded as
King's College in 1440 by
Henry VI for seventy
scholars. It has grown over
the centuries to become the
best known public school in
the land. The king also
founded King's College,
Cambridge which was built in
a similar style.

FINGEST

The Norman tower of St
Bartholomew's Church, with
its twin saddleback roof, is a
rare example of this type of
architecture. Fingest, set high
in the Hambleden Valley,
takes its name from the old
Danish word meaning
'meeting place'. In the village
are many attractive cottages,
some timber-framed.

GERRARD'S CROSS

The brick-built Pigeon House
stands in the grounds of
Bulstrode Park, a former
stately home which is now the
headquarters of a world
religious organization.
Gerrard's Cross has grown in
recent years and its position
between the M40 and the M25
motorways places it firmly in
the London commuter belt.

GORING

Gabled boathouses with balconies line the Thames at Goring. Attractively placed between the wooded hills of the Chilterns and the Berkshire Downs, Goring has become a fashionable place to live.

GREAT MISSENDEN

Sheep grazing in a Chiltern valley near the parish church at Great Missenden. This quiet village has grown in recent years but still manages to keep its tranquil atmosphere.

GREAT HAMPDEN

Hampden House was the home of John Hampden who defied Charles I over 'ship money' and was a renowned Parliamentarian. He died in battle during the Civil War and is buried, with many of his ancestors, in the nearby church.

HADDENHAM

Roses growing over garden fences in a quiet corner of Haddenham.

HADDENHAM

Ducks on the village pond beside the green. Many of the walls in the village are topped with thatch and local lore has it that the pond once had a thatched cover to keep the ducks dry. Although the village has grown, the older parts still retain a traditional atmosphere.

HAMBLEDEN

The Manor House in the centre of the village is the home of the Hambleden family and dates from the early seventeenth century. It is built of flint and brick and has high gables in a traditional style.

HAMBLEDEN

Nestling in a valley
surrounded by mature trees of
oak and beech, this must be
one of the most idyllic
settings for a village. The
square tower of the village
church rising above the red
tiled roofs of the cottages and
the tall, gabled manor house
make Hambleden much
sought after by film makers
looking for a 'typical English
village'.

HAMBLEDEN

Mill End near Hambleden
a fine June day seen here
the weir where a footpath
stretches across the river f
the old mill to Hambleden
Lock.

HARPSDEN

One of several farm buildings decorated with old wooden, wallpaper printing blocks; an unusual feature in this small hamlet near Henley-on-Thames.

HENLEY-ON-THAMES

A view from the tower of the parish church during regatta week. The regatta, held in mid-summer, attracts oarsmen from all over the world and is one of the high spots of the social season. Next to the bridge can be seen the new and modern-looking headquarters for the regatta.

HENLEY-ON-THAMES

The regatta has been held on the Thames since 1839. Starting here at Temple Island, crews row down one of the straightest stretches of the river, finishing just before Henley Bridge. What began as a one day event of three races has gradually expanded to become a week's sporting endeavour watched by thousands from the towpath. Many go to be seen as much as to see.

HIGH WYCOMBE

Castle Place in the centre of High Wycombe, squeezed between the parish church and the railway line, is one of the few surviving parts of the original town. In recent years much of the centre has been demolished to make way for shops and roads.

HIGH WYCOMBE

The High Street boasts several fine buildings; the Market Hall seen here, and the Guildhall, are two particularly good examples. The Market Hall was rebuilt by Robert Adam in 1761 and although the building itself is no longer used for its original purpose the area around it is still the scene of weekly markets.

HUGHENDEN

The impressive, red brick Hughenden Manor was the country home of Benjamin Disraeli who rebuilt the house and gardens after he purchased them in 1847. Now open to the public, many visitors are attracted to this home of one of Queen Victoria's best-loved Prime Ministers.

HURLEY

A summer's day on the Thames as a mother and daughter fish for tiddlers in the shallow waters and canoeists enjoy a day's sport. The river with its lock and nearby caravan park attracts many visitors.

HURLEY

St Mary's Church is all that remains of an ancient Benedictine Priory, founded in 1087.

JORDANS

This Friends Meeting House attracts a steady flow of visitors, many of them American, to see the final resting place of William Penn, the founder of Pennsylvania. Jordans is still an important centre for the Friends or Quakers as they are more usually known.

THE LEE

Cottages on the village green in this small hamlet high above the beechwoods on the scarp of the Chilterns. The name Lee comes from the old English placename *leah* meaning a clearing in the woods.

THE LEE

This unusual sight of a wooden ship's figurehead is in the front garden of Pipers, the home of the Liberty family. Timber from the ship from which the figurehead came was used in the building of Liberty's famous store in Regent Street, London. The figure represents Admiral Howe.

LEWKNOR

The churchyard and church of St Margaret in this hamlet on the edge of the Chilterns, close to the busy M40 motorway. The original church dates from the twelfth and thirteenth centuries and has stained-glass windows designed by William Morris.

MAIDENHEAD

Since early Victorian times
Boulter's Lock has attracted
visitors to this Thames-side
town to enjoy the river.
Elegant gowns and boater hats
on slowly moving punts were
once the order of the day,
now powered launches
dominate the river.

MAIDENHEAD

A summer's day on the
Thames near Maidenhead
where visitors feed the swans.
This is the time of year when
the traditional 'swan-upping' –
the counting and marking of
swans – takes place along the
river.

MARLOW

Marlow's traditional image is of a sleepy, historic Thames-side town but around its outskirts are several industrial estates with modern buildings like this one.

MARLOW

The tall elegant spire of Saints Church can be see through one of the arch of the famous suspensio bridge. Not so widely k is that it was built by W Clark who constructed t famous bridge over the Danube, linking the onc separate cities of Buda a Pest.

MARLOW

The traditional riverside house reflected in the still waters of the mill cut, contrasts sharply with the modern buildings behind, which were built on the site of the old mill.

MARSWORTH

An image of this timber-framed cottage is reflected in the quiet waters of the Grand Union Canal. The colourful canal boats in the background remind us of a time when the canal was crowded with commercial boats, before the coming of the railway.

NETTLEBED

This tall kiln is all that now remains of a thriving brickmaking industry in Nettlebed, which dates back to the early fifteenth century. Once a busy coaching stop, Nettlebed still has many fine inns and coaching buildings in the High Street.

PANGBOURNE

The iron bridge across the Thames, linking Pangbourne with Whitchurch, was built in Victorian times and is one of several toll bridges on the river. Pangbourne has some interesting riverside houses and a famous nautical college.

PENN

Great oak trees stand beside a field near Penn seen here on a late autumn day. The nearby village takes its name from the great Quaker, William Penn, founder of the state of Pennsylvania.

PITSTONE

Pitstone Windmill, one of the oldest post mills in the country is owned by the National Trust and stands on the edge of the Chiltern escarpment. The nearby church of St Mary is noted for its Norman font and Jacobean pulpit, both fine examples of their kind.

PRINCES RISBOROUGH

Flowers bloom outside the town hall, a good example of nineteenth-century civic architecture. Princes Risborough, now a busy, modern, agricultural town, can also boast nearby Saxon earthworks, a Norman church and a fine old manor house. A recently built ring road has greatly reduced traffic in this attractive market square.

RADNAGE

The church of St Mary with its square Norman tower stands between several small hamlets collectively called Radnage. For many years a massive bier, dated 1699, was kept in the church and used to carry villagers to their final resting place.

RADNAGE

A sunny day among harvest fields in the Chilterns near Radnage. Here farmland gives way to forestry and the beechwoods which are such a feature of the area and mainstay of its local industry.

RYCOTE

The chapel of St Michael was founded in 1449 by the Lord of the Manor, Richard Quartermaine and his wife Sybil, and was originally used as a chantry chapel. Its particular interest is that it was all built at one time and has never been altered. It is noted for its seventeenth century fittings, including a pew believed to have been set up for the visit of Charles I to Rycote in 1625.

SONNING

Reflected in the waters of the Thames on a sunny summer day is the brick-built bridge at Sonning. This is a rare, peaceful moment on the river which for most of the summer is crowded with pleasure craft.

STOKE ROW

What looks like a bandstand is, in fact, the cover to a well given to the village in 1863 by the Maharajah of Benares, when he heard that there was no water supply to this small community. A cast-iron, gold painted elephant stands above the machinery for drawing water.

STOKENCHURCH

A frosty winter afternoon in beechwoods near Stokenchurch. Near here is a sculpture trail recently opened by the Forestry Commission.

STONOR PARK

The main entrance to Stonor Park with spectacular carvings and semi-circular steps is only one of the features of this magnificent house. Others include a number of priest holes which in earlier centuries may have been made use of by the Stonors, an old Roman Catholic family.

STONOR PARK

The house and private chapel at Stonor Park, home of the Stonor family since at least the twelfth century. Set in its own picturesque valley, the park is also home to a large herd of deer.

THAME

A view through the gateway into the courtyard of the Old Grammar School, founded by Lord Williams of Thame in 1558 and now used as offices. Lord Williams's coat of arms is carved over the doorway.

THAME

In a town noted for its timber-framed buildings, this one, close to the church, is a particularly good example. Thame has been an important market town since the thirteenth century. The High Street, where the market was held until 1950, is very long and wide with a number of picturesque old inns and private houses.

THAME

Although the outskirts of Thame have spread greatly in recent years there are still some peaceful spots on the banks of the river Thame from which to fish. Nor has the town moved too far from its rural roots since it still stages, in September, one of the largest one-day agricultural shows in the country – an occasion for an extra local school holiday.

TRING

In the woods near Tring a charcoal burner plies his ancient trade. For centuries the woods of the Chilterns have provided a living for those prepared to undertake this hard and dirty work. Although numbers have declined greatly in recent times, there are still a few who carry on this traditional skill.

TURVILLE

Sunshine illuminates the stained-glass window in St Mary's Church, Turville. The church also has several examples of armorial glass of the sixteenth and eighteenth centuries.

TURVILLE

There can be few more charming rural scenes than in this village with its old church and churchyard, country cottages and windmill. The latter has featured in many films and is now a private house.

WALLINGFORD

A winter's day beside the Thames at Wallingford. This quiet scene belies the fact that this is now a town with around 7,000 inhabitants, which has developed rapidly in recent years. There has been a Thames crossing here since at least the time of William the Conqueror.

WARGRAVE

A grand riverside house on the banks of the Thames below the Henley to Wargrave road, near Conway's Bridge. The narrow bridge, built in the eighteenth century is hardly wide enough for the volume of modern traffic which now passes over it.

WARGRAVE

High society may make for Henley but Wargrave, like many riverside villages, stages its own more local affair. The regatta apart, another point of interest about Wargrave is that its church was burnt down in 1914, apparently as a protest, by the suffragettes.

WEST WYCOMBE

The church of St Lawrence
with its conspicuous golden
ball overlooks the village of
West Wycombe. The golden
ball was provided for the
church in the eighteenth
century by Sir Francis
Dashwood, founder of the
notorious Hell Fire Club.

WEST WYCOMBE

This mausoleum next to the
church has been the burial
place for members of the
Dashwood family since the
mid-eighteenth century. Made
of flint, it is hexagonal and
open to the sky.

WINDSOR

The tower of Windsor Castle looks across the river Thames to Eton College boatyard. In an age of fibreglass river craft, this boatyard still produces traditionally made wooden boats.